Here And Not Forgotten

Here And Not Forgotten

Stories Of A Wiser Generation

Drew Feith Tye
Introduction by Larry Kane
Photography by Jordan Cassway

To order additional copies of this book, contact:
Xlibris Corporation
1-888-795-4274
www.Xlibris.com
Orders@Xlibris.com
68915

To my family and Reuben:
Thank you for being my best audience.
I love you very much.

TABLE OF CONTENTS

"Old places and old persons in their turn, when spirit dwells in them, have an intrinsic vitality of which youth is incapable, precisely, the balance and wisdom that come from long perspectives and broad foundations."

-George Santayana, philosopher, poet, and humanist (1863-1952)

"Seek ye counsel of the aged, for their eyes have looked on the faces of the years and their ears have hearkened to the voices of Life. Even if their counsel is displeasing to you, pay heed to them."

-Kalil Gibran, artist, poet, and writer (1883-1931)

"Look, I don't want to wax philosophic, but I will say that if you're alive you've got to flap your arms and legs, you've got to jump around a lot, for life is the very opposite of death, and therefore you must at very least think noisy and colorfully, or you're not alive."

-Mel Brooks, film director, screenwriter, composer, lyricist, comedian, actor, and producer (1926-   )

ACKNOWLEDGEMENTS

Many people assisted me in the making of this book.

Thank you to the Madlyn and Leonard Abramson Center for Jewish Life, specifically President and CEO Carol Irvine, Director of Annual Giving Joy Gordon, Director of Volunteers Mona Gold, and Senior Communications Specialist Patti Tuberty, for your insightful advice and continuous support. You encouraged me to pursue this project to my creative heart's content, and I am forever indebted to you for the experience.

I would like to extend my deepest gratitude to Larry Kane, who has served as so much more than a contributor to this book. You are as much my mentor as a paternal figure, and I would likely be lost without your guidance and unrelenting encouragement.

Thank you so much to Jordan Cassway, photographer extraordinaire. Your experience and creative vision took this book to a whole new level, and it was a thrill to share sarcastic comments with you.

I would also like to extend a very special thank you to Erika Garcia, Simone Rodriquez, Lani Meyer, and my Xlibris Publishing Team. You are the reason this book came to life in print, and I am so lucky to have been able to work with you.

And last but certainly not least, thank you to Lilly, Esther, Samson, Sylvia, Gertrude, Herman, Milton, and Gene. Your voices and candid storytelling filled this book with inspiration, life, and love.

INTRODUCTION
By Larry Kane

The memory of a long lost lover or friend. Regrets over decisions made and decisions deferred. Life lessons learned through adversity, glory, success, and failure. The bonds of family, the grips of despair, and the deep, dark scars of the greatest mass murder in history.

As a newsman, I thrive by reading other people's stories, but when you search the epic moments of a person's life, can you learn from it? Can you seek guidance and solace and vision? Or, if you prefer, is it just someone's story, a person who will never become part of genuine history? And the question remains—is there value in one person's story, the same value you assign to the historical record of a nation or a King or a President?

The answer is a resounding "Yes", because in the end, it is individuals who create history with their courage and determination to secure a better life for themselves and their survivors.

It is this sense of the importance and lessons of personal history that drive the stories researched and written by Drew Feith Tye with the proud citizens of the Abramson Center. These personal accounts are positive proof that we can learn from an individual's past, so much in fact, that they may illuminate our own future.

These stories will make you laugh, make you cry, and lead you to wonder whether you are living your life to the fullest and embracing the most precious gift—time itself. I find them fascinating, instructive, and memorable, and I know you will, too.

FOREWORD

The elderly are entirely underrated and underestimated.

Before embarking on this project, the only older people I *truly* knew were my mom's parents, my Bubby and Zayda, and my Mimi, my dad's mother. I knew their quirks, the foods they loved to eat, the clothes they always wore, and the stories they liked to tell. I knew their values, the lessons they taught, the manner in which they dealt with grief, the way they expressed happiness.

The same was not true of the following eight interviewees.

Lilly, Esther, Samson, Sylvia, Gertrude, Herman, Milton, and Gene were all strangers to me, at first. The Abramson Center Staff, who assured me that I would learn a great deal from each of these individuals, recommended them for this project.

Their selections were undeniably captivating.

I approached each interview as an assignment and left with more than just their stories—I left with a real part of each of them; a part of their hearts, minds, and spirits that they were so generously willing to share. I learned about their childhoods, the importance of Judaism in their lives, the jobs they held, and the challenges they faced. I learned about their parents and siblings and children, the way they met their spouses, the way their spouses died.

I was given a glimpse into more than 714 years of life experience.

Like my grandparents, each of them bestowed upon me something different—two showed me their musical talents, one his abstract, stunning artwork. One described her liberating life as an independent woman, one reflected on her still-thriving relationship with her ninety-seven-year-old brother. One taught me about how his passion for the stock market keeps him invested in life, and two revealed their horrific recollections of their young lives during the Holocaust and the very different attitudes they now possess.

Age may bring similar exterior changes to everyone, but what's inside is always distinct.

Each story revealed different textures, colors, and patterns, and together created a quilted illustration of a generation rooted in dedication to family, perseverance in work, and an overall practical view of life. As Herman says in his interview: "I did not think of myself as anything special. I did what I had to do."

My Zayda always said: "When you leave this world, the only thing you leave behind is your legacy." The following eight stories reflect legacies still being created.

LILLIAN TAUS
Age: 86

I don't think I'm cut out for this.

I spend the entire morning nervously mulling over my interview questions and dreading my first conversation with a resident of the Center. What if they think I am presumptuous? What if I can't hear them or they can't hear me and I'll have to scream and the interview won't go anywhere? I convince myself that nothing can go horribly wrong, take one last look at the list of names, and walk down the hallway to the Abramson Inn.

Lilly is seated in the middle of two women in the dining hall. I approach her, and before I can say more than a "Hello", Lilly reaches for my hand and holds it in hers. "Hello, Sweetheart" she says. Her hair is a light blonde, her face is a delicate, creamy vanilla, and her eyes are green and kind. "I'm Lilly. They told me you were coming to talk to me." Immediately I feel better. She seems happy to see me—pleased about the conversation we are about to have. "Come, come dear, to my apartment."

I sit down at the small kitchen table next to the Kitchenette, only to rise seconds later to look at her pictures on the dresser and wall of the living room. "You must have so many stories about your family," I say as we sit back down at the table. "I'll tell you everything—no secrets, because it's true."

"When I was born, [my country] was called Czech and Russia took it over. Then the war started so Hungarians took over the country and I had to learn every language and I talked six languages." Already, Lilly impresses me. This small woman, no taller than five foot flat, juggled six complicated languages in her teenage years.

Lilly explains how her knowledge of language served as an immediate advantage during the Nazi occupation: "And then the Germans came in so I speak German, so it saved my life because when the transfer came to Auschwitz, they called me always to translate. I was useful all the time and this way I saved my sister." Imagine a language helping you to save a family member. Lilly never knew before that the German language would be so important.

I ask Lilly about her sister, and she beams (this is the first of many surprisingly light moments during our discussion). "My sister is eighty now and she was eleven [when we were taken away]." Lilly pauses to think for a moment and remembers a story about how her persistent efforts helped save her sister: "[My sister] got sick. She got typhoid in Auschwitz and I met a lady. She was the nurse—a Jewish woman and I told her: 'What shall I do? I want to save my sister that's the only thing I have—I'm the child of thirteen children help me please, help me.' Anyhow she had pity on me and she brought me an aspirin everyday to give my sister and I saved her life." It is impossible for me to understand the kind of terror she must have faced—even asking another Jewish woman to help her. Anything could happen to anyone at anytime.

I ask Lilly about the rest her family, and the light in her face dims to a sad, deep gray. "They went straight to the gas chambers. My mother had a two-year-old baby in her hand—someone said to her [in Yiddish] 'You're only thirty-eight years old, you can live but the baby cannot live'—the Jewish boys who helped them unload the cart said this to her and my mother said 'Meschugenne! He told me to throw my flesh and blood away, how could I do that? What kind of Jewish man is he?' She didn't know what was going on. So she says 'I'm not going to throw my child away, it's my flesh and blood', and this is how she went straight into the gas chamber." I don't know how Lilly is able to recount this vivid horror, but she does without hesitation. My chest hardens as I imagine what runs through her mind at this moment.

"What about your father?" I ask. "Did he also go to the gas chamber?" "No." she says. "My father was in Dachau. He was a kosher butcher so he worked in the kitchen and got enough food to help nourish other people—he was very useful for everyone." The thought of her father surviving relaxes me.

"The day of liberation he ate something and dropped dead."

"What was your life like before the camp?" I jump at the chance to turn to a lighter subject. "As a child, when I was thirteen my father says 'Kind [child in Yiddish], you have a head on your shoulders, you gonna grow up to be something. How about if I sent you to Bratislava to go to Jewish school and learn something?' so I went and I lived with my Bubby."

Lilly smiles as she continues: "But my Aunt went to Prague to get papers to come to America and then when she came back she said: 'Do you know your mother is going to have another child?' and I said 'Oh my god! So what shall I do?' and I can't tell my Bubby, so I decided I'm gonna get up in the morning and I would go home—my mother needs me more than my education. [My education is] not important." Lilly's love for her family is evident. "But I didn't have money to go home, so I sit the whole time on the toilet all the way home so when everyone went down, I went down, too!" I can just picture her as a young, beautiful little girl, crouching down on the closed toilet seat, praying no one would come to kick her off the train.

"So I came home and two weeks later my mother started having the baby—she said: 'Go and knock on the door of this and this woman she's a midwife and this and this a midwife and come quick because I feel the baby is coming.' So I did that but no one was home—I come home and my mother says the baby's coming and she said: 'Take a scissor and take warm water and shamatas [rags]' and I was only fourteen years old—so I had delivered the baby!" I gasp at the thought of the stress and pain and ignorance of a young girl watching her mother open up and give birth to a child. "When it came to cut the cord she says 'Cut this' but I said 'No!' and I run from the room—I won't hurt my mother—but she says 'Give me the scissors'." "YOU LET HER CUT IT *HERSELF*?" I yell. "Nooo, no. I didn't let her do it herself she said to me: 'It doesn't hurt it has to come out,' so I had no choice so I cut it and I put it in a towel and washed it off and it was a little boy." Lilly lets out the same breath of relief she must have after that moment over seventy years before.

"How many siblings did you have?" I ask. Families were big back then, so I'm not surprised to hear her response. "Lemme see now . . . we were eight girls and five boys. I was the oldest." Then without any prompt, Lilly moves into a story about her husband. "When I came to this country my husband was a barber. I was jealous because he's making money and I'm doing nothing—I'm with my baby—so I put her in a nursery and I worked with him. But I was ok, they liked me." Lilly showed me a picture of her daughter when we entered her apartment. I'm curious about her. "We were in Germany—my daughter was born in 1947. Rita is a diamond, you never saw anything like it." I smile—that's what my own Bubby would say about my mom. "I will never die for hunger because she takes such good care of me."

Lilly tells me that her husband's name was Morris. "How did you meet him?" I ask. Lilly lights up again. I love hearing these kinds of stories, and she obviously loves talking about it.

"Well if I tell you, you wont believe that that could happen . . ."

"The day of liberation we were five girls kept together—I didn't even know we were so naïve, misht—so we had one blanket for the five of us and we escaped into the woods and we spread out the blanket and we laid down for the night—thank G-d no planes, no shootings, nothing." I can just picture them—five painfully thin, strangely happy young women snuggled on a small dirty blanket after escaping. I wonder if the air tasted different. It must have.

"So, all of a sudden the bugs started biting us on the floor! So we got up and all of a sudden we see a man running so we got scared we thought he was a German so we start running the other way and all of a sudden he starts speaking Yiddish. He says: 'Maydelekh vi lofyt itzt? Ikh bin a Yid!'" From taking Yiddish, I understood him to say: "Little girl, where do you run now? I am a Jew!"

"My husband," Lilly says.

I can't believe it. That man was Morris. "That's how I met him. He says: 'Why are you laying here on the floor? You're gonna get sick—you could come in with me to a German house—all of the Germans left—and you can sleep in a house, in a bed', and he helped all the five of us. He was such a good human being, a mentsch. A gute neshuma [a good soul]."

Lilly continues: "So then he took us in and we slept there and then in the morning he brought us breakfast and took us to a place to take a shower, and he got us clothes because we only had those stripes—no panties, no bras, nothing, and wooden shoes." I ask Lilly if Morris was wearing the stripes, too, and she said "No".

"He didn't wear the stripes because he was a barber and he worked for the S.S.—he shaved and cut the hair of Jews so he had it good in the concentration camp." 'Had it good?' I can't understand it. The term 'good' took on a warped meaning during that time. I ask Lilly if Morris ever talked about his experiences in the camp. "He talked about it, but he was happy because he got plenty of food and he helped other people—he had a brother there and everyone had enough food and they liked him so much that they gave him meat, potatoes, and soup and he gave it to the Jewish boys and they were very happy to have him as a friend." Morris truly was a good soul.

Lilly tells me about Morris's past before the camp: "He lived in Poland. They were nine children. Only one brother was left—an older brother—he was a tailor, a very good tailor and he was married but I never knew his wife. After the war was over, he went to Poland to look for his two-year-old little girl named Lucy and he found her." It's like something I've heard in a movie—going back and finding a child that was abandoned years before. Lilly assures me this is all true. "Lucy was there and when they took her mother to Auschwitz the mother said to the neighbor: 'I'm not going to survive I know. Please take my child. Someone is going to pick her up after the war', so that neighbor raised her—Lucy was four years old when the war was over—and the father came and picked her up and the lady didn't want to give Lucy up to him and they had to go to the Jewish Gemynde and he said, 'This is my child' so finally he got the child. He brought her to my house and she stayed there for five years."

Lilly brings the story to the present: "She lives in Texas now and I even introduced her to a young man—a schitakh [a matchmaking]—and they are married and they have children—they are very well keyn eyn-hore ["no evil eye" or "thank goodness"], and her husband was an accountant and he gave up accounting after they were married and opened up a grocery store then he wound up building houses for the Mexican people and they became rich. So I've been there and stayed there and watched their children. They have a son and a daughter." Life goes on. Lilly knows this better than most people. She gets up from the table and rummages around the living room, trying to find a picture of Lucy with Elie Weisel. She can't find it and assumes her daughter took it to show someone.

I ask Lilly what her experience was like in the camp. "In Auschwitz I always got busy—let's say the Shtubmeltz [I'm assuming she's referring to a German woman who worked in the camp] she said, 'You know how to cook?' 'I know how to cook. I'll do whatever you want.' I need food to feed my sister so I had it good and I helped other people, too. Whoever I could help, I tried." Lilly reveals an amazing story about one particular woman with whom she was friendly: "I was in twenty-nine block and a woman was in thirty who was a friend of mine, and I said: 'How 'bout if I pick up the soup the dead people don't eat and I'll bring it to your people to survive?' and I did that and she didn't know how to reciprocate so she took a blanket—it was winter, cold weather—and cut off a piece and made a belt and put it together and I wore it. My job at that time was to pull out the dead bodies, put a number on them and put them in the high snow—all of a sudden the Obersheft (the highest German in the S.S.) he says: 'Who gave you the right to take German property and cut it up and make yourself comfortable and warm?'" Lilly couldn't tell him that it came from her friend, so she tried to convince him that she took it off of one of the dead bodies and put it on herself. He became very angry with her and demanded that she come to his office later that day. When she told her sister what had happened, they both cried because they thought she was going to be killed. She went to his office and told him that he could have the piece of cloth even though it was disgusting and dirty, and he believed her and sent her back. When she got back, her sister saw her and cried again out of desperate relief.

Lilly rests her arm on the table. I look down. No numbers. I ask her why. "I helped build an airport for the Germans. My sister was there, too. Every so often, they'd take the weak people who couldn't work to the gas chambers. My sister was sick so they took her and I went with her. We arrived at the doors to the gas chambers and the German there he said: 'Why did you bring these shaizer [shit] here today? It's Sunday.'" That Sunday happened to be a German holiday, so the Germans weren't working. This coincidence saved their lives. "So we saw a line of people who were waiting for bread, so we snuck in line and got our bread." I suppose that Lilly would have gotten numbers if she didn't sneak away from the Germans every chance she got.

"G-d gave me the strength to help others," she says as she leans back in her chair. Her walls are covered with awards of all kinds for her work with Jewish National Fund, Holocaust Survivor foundations, and numerous other organizations involving Israel. She shows me her big plastic bucket filled with soda pop-tops that she collects from other residents to send to the JNF to raise money. She tells me about the Tzedaka boxes she gives to her friends to raise money for other Jewish organizations. She explains how she visits other Holocaust survivors or lonely people in the Center who don't receive many visitors and brings them candy and fruit and other goodies to make them happy. Lilly does it all.

But Lilly misses Morris desperately. I ask gently how Morris died. "It's been two and a half years now. Morris wanted to go back to Poland to see where he was born. I didn't want to go—I wasn't from Poland—but he went back and he brought Lucy with him. When they were walking around, he was approached by a German Shepard dog; one that reminded him of the dogs that attacked Jews at the camp. It did something to him. When he returned he got very sick and was stricken with Alzheimer's. It was very bad from then on until he died."

Under all of her spirit of survival, her endless selflessness, and her ability to share her story over and over (Lilly has been in Spielberg's *Shoah* film and spoke at many colleges), she is human. Her eyes bother her, she is frustrated by the slow-growing tomato garden behind her apartment, and she needs the night table in her bedroom switched with the side table in her living room. Lilly's humanity makes her most impressive, and we have become very good friends. I take her to the eye doctor in the Center, she promises me tomatoes when they grow, and I make sure the maintenance staff move her tables. Lilly has become like a grandmother to me, and I am here for her just like she is for everyone else.

ESTHER CANE
Age: 83

I enter the apartment to find an elderly woman seated alone on a couch, knitting. Her silk, billowy blouse is painted with muted purples and gray lines and tightens at her wrists. Her hair is short, slightly unkempt perhaps from her sleep the night before. Only the natural light from the large window sets the room with a gray glow. "Esther?" I ask. I know it's she but I don't want to be too forward and assume she knows who I am. I introduce myself as I step closer, and she looks confused at my request. "I'd like to interview you, if that's OK." "What do you want to know?" She asks, her throaty accent cutting the silence in the room. "About your life, your experiences," I continue. "I went through hell in my life," she says. "Sit down."

"We were seven kids . . . my brothers first and then I came and so on and so on. So whenever I went to play with my friends I always had a baby with me!" We begin laughing, and the stillness warms. Esther takes long pauses and often repeats herself without realizing. "I have three sons . . . after three sons I said to my husband 'The shop is closed! It's not Europe here, our kids need education.'" Esther clearly has a great sense of humor, and laughter makes the entire interview easier for both of us.

Esther describes the role of Judaism in her childhood: "I went to private school my father made a good living—I went to Hebrew School. Judaism was an important part of my childhood—when the Shabbos came we were not allowed to make a fire so a gentile woman came and she made the fire you know on the stove, and she boiled the soup and she cooked for Saturday, too, and so on." She stops speaking and breathes deeply.

"I went through hell in my life."

"Tell me about that," I ask. It is a risk, but I hope she wants to talk. She breathes deeply again. "The Germans came into Poland and the beginning was not too bad—this was 1939." We are getting somewhere, somewhere significant. Then she stops again. "It's hard." I can feel her retreating, wanting to quit. My Zayda survived the Holocaust and never spoke of his experiences, and I certainly am not going to push Esther to say anything. "You don't have to talk if you don't want to," I reassure her. But something has come over her that urges her from the inside—an urge that causes her to reveal her story and her forearm.

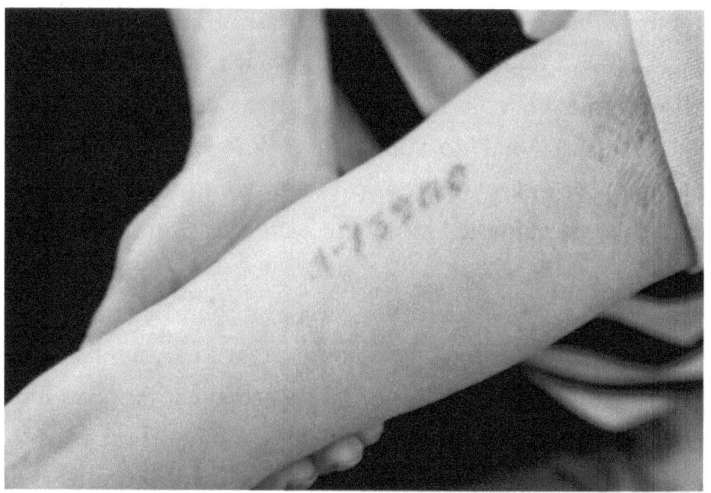

"I was in Auschwitz," she says, aggressively rolling up her silk sleeve to reveal a letter "A" followed by a series of numbers. "'A' was for women, 'B' was for men, and 'C' was for gypsies. Germans said 'tsgoyne' which means gypsies." Other residents and staff told me that Esther always shows her numbers to people—as if she wants the "show-and-tell" to be a constant reminder of the terror she endured—a force that will hopefully keep people from forgetting what happened.

"So what happened to you?" I ask, leaning in closer.

"Hmm. The Germans came to Poland and separated the women from the men. They took the men and locked them up in the synagogue, and the women and the children were sent out of the house, and I pushed myself to the front [of the crowd] and I had my little sister—you know we were seven kids!" I can picture this scene—a crowd of screaming and confusion. Imagine not knowing anything about what is happening or what is about to happen to you and your entire family. Imagine how much we know now. If only it could have been different.

"I had long black hair and made platz [braids] around my head I guess [the Germans] liked that. I was the first one to be selected to go the concentration camp." Her voice has a sad pride—it is as if she had a real place in the crowd, a strange role that she will never forget. "I didn't know—there was another truck connected with another truck, he said 'Go to the other truck with the other mothers.' He tells me to go, I went, and I came to the door and my sister started crying and I started crying, too. The German came over and started kicking my sister with his boot, and started kicking me in my coccyx bone, and I felt it until after the war." She reaches behind her to touch her lower back. Her own physical touch startles her. " . . . and I got up—oy vey, I don't remember nothing." Esther is overcome with emotion, but I try to keep her going, still afraid that I will upset her. "Do you remember being at the camp?" I ask quietly. "Oh yes, I remember."

Esther's memory might relapse at times throughout the interview, but certain details are so clear that I feel in this amazing way Esther has brought me into her experience, into Auschwitz. What a horrible feeling—so real to her and so incomprehensible to me.

"The German police was a section and I worked for them. I helped a gentile Polish woman—she cooked for them, but [the Polish] don't cook like Jews!" We laugh and, like it did before, the comfortable chuckles help her to continue: "I washed the dishes, washed the floor." "How did you get chosen to do these things?" I ask. I had heard of people being saved by the jobs they were given, but I never understood how it happened. "I don't know [why they chose me to do these jobs]. It was just luck." Luck—a thread that ties all survivors together. Esther keeps talking and describes a memory that brings laughter to her bleak recollections.

"[The Germans] shot the gooses, you know, the wild gooses, and they brought them back [to the kitchen]. I had to work, and the German soldier said 'We brought two gooses and [the gentile woman] didn't come to work' and so I said 'Don't worry, I'll fix it.' And so I took off the feathers, opened up the goose and took out the livers and made chopped liver! I made chopped liver, took the gooses in the oven and put in apples, sewed them up, and I took chicken legs and thighs and made a chicken soup with lokshen [noodles] and lima beans. Jewish food for the Germans!"

I try to envision this bizarre image in my mind. It's almost too surreal to believe.

Esther continues. "[The Germans] said: 'What is that?' 'Delicious!' I said. 'You taste it!' [One of the Germans] said, because he thought I maybe poisoned it. They started eating, and they loved it! They ate everything but the potatoes they left. After they finished eating, I went to the camp and took my food." Esther used one of her most treasured Jewish activities—cooking—to save her life. She never thought that cooking would serve such a purpose, and her cooking put her at an incredible advantage over others in the camp. "[After a while], they said: 'You're not going to go to the camp kitchen, you're going to eat here' so I cooked more, and my father, my two brothers, and my uncle (my father's youngest brother) were digging ditches [in the same camp] to put in water. When they finished [their work], I went out and gave [food] to them."

At that time, Esther was seventeen years old.

"'Where did you learn to cook like this?' one of the Germans asked me. 'I learned from my mother. I was my mothers helper.' I said." She looks at me and raises her eyebrows. The irony of his question is horrific. "They never asked me anything else ever again, because they knew my mother was dead."

The following story reveals another dimension of Esther's experience cooking for the Germans.

"The Germans were not plain Germans they were officers. They watched over the area. They were nice to me because I cooked for them. The Polish gentile woman who cooked for them didn't come in for a while because I think she was pregnant. One of the Germans [who I cooked for] came over to me and asked me, 'How old are you?' I said 'Seventeen'. He wanted to rape me, and he came at me, so I screamed bloody murder. That area had a tailor, a shoemaker, all Jews, all for the Germans. The shoemaker came running because he heard me screaming, he thought maybe I burned myself because I was working the kitchen. 'Who sent for you?!' [The German said]. 'I thought she burned herself!' The soldier never touched me again."

Esther believes that the Polish gentile woman got pregnant from this same man. "You must have been relieved that the tailor came to save you!" I say. Esther's response reveals a profound truth that helps me to try to understand her perspective: "I was not a happy person—whatever I got, I was satisfied. Happy people didn't exist." Her life as a simple teenage girl was changed forever.

"They shot my family to death," Esther says, her voice shaking. "The whole world stood still, didn't lift a finger to help us."

"The Germans went to Russia and they froze to death and they started losing the war. You never heard a history like that."

I ask Esther if she told her children about what had happened to her. "I didn't want my kids to worry about it so I never told them [about my past when they were young]. I couldn't escape it—they used to ask me: 'Mom, what is that on your arm?' But I said: 'When you get older, I'll tell you.' All of my sons know." Esther wanted to provide her children with the protection she herself didn't have.

I ask Esther whether or not she believes in G-d. "No," she says. "Where was G-d? When I was in the camp, where was He? Where was He when we needed Him?" I don't have an answer. I don't know what to say.

SAMSON EISENBERG
Age: 94

As I stand in the doorway of Samson apartment, I can't tell if he likes me, nevertheless wants me to interview him. His wide, blue eyes and small, pursed mouth are hard to interpret. I knock gingerly on his open doorframe, hoping that he will remember my bright orange sweater and my face from a few hours before when we made our appointment to meet. "Hi, Samson" I say as I tiptoe into the room. "Hi," he says, without much exclamation. "Sit down."

Samson Eisenberg was born in Philadelphia on October 15th, 1914, as one of eight children. His parents were from Russia and Austria. While we talk, he turns from his electric wheelchair to point at an old, gray picture on his wall. "You see that picture of the six boys? That's me and my brothers." I squint to make out the faces—they all look alike, and are arranged in two rows, each swarthy, their mouths painted with a serious expression. "We played in an orchestra together, and I played the saxophone and clarinet." He then points to two separate pictures of his sisters. "They were very good schoolteachers."

"I love music," he tells me, "mostly classical and jazz but really anything, and I played [those instruments] when I was twelve years old until I was seventeen years old." Samson sang with his brothers in different choirs for many years. He belonged to Beth Sholom Congregation and Keneseth Israel Congregation in Elkins Park, Pennsylvania. "I grew up in an ultra-Orthodox home," he says, pointing to a picture of a young man draped in a talis, his right hand gripping a shofar. "That's my father." Though he is no longer Orthodox, Judaism was and is a very important part of Samson's life.

When he was seventeen, Samson met his first wife, Dorothy. As I ask him questions about her, his initial seriousness melts away slightly—as if he is comfortable with her name swirling around in the air of his small apartment. "We met at Hebrew High School where we both attended. She was a year younger than me," he says. "We were married a year later." His face reveals a small smile—"The wedding took place at her home, and during the ceremony, my mother held a candle too close to Dorothy's veil, and it caught fire!" We laugh together for a moment. "There's always something," he says, his smile hardening a little. "No matter what, you can't please everyone." Samson tells me another funny story: "My granddaughter got married in California. It was on this cliff, and when her husband stepped on the glass, it slipped so far away from him it flew over the cliff! Then, when he tried it a second time, he stepped on her foot." The parallels of the generations made sweet connections in his head. "I'll tell you," he says, his lips curling up like the first peel of a lemon. "There's always something."

The tone turns somber as we return to Dorothy. "My wife eventually had breast cancer and passed away. We were married sixty years." I ask if they were happy, and he looks very sure of himself. "When she was sick, I used to take her to the casinos in Atlantic City—she loved the distraction of all of the people, and the motion of playing the slots. It was good for her, and I was happy to do it." I could tell how much he cared for her. "It was her therapy."

Samson held many jobs as a younger man. He worked in home improvement for forty years, and before that, he worked at the Ward Baking Company making bread and cake for ten years. "I loved to work," he says, "and though two of my brothers were doctors and one was a dentist, I prided myself on being the 'black sheep' of the family." I laugh. I love that expression, and I've never heard it out of the mouth of a ninety-four-year-old.

Dorothy and Samson had two children, Renee and Harvey. Renee is a schoolteacher, a counselor, and is proficient in music (especially the piano), and Harvey is a famous angio-radiologist. Samson beams while talking about his kids. "My son lives in Newport Beach, California, and was involved in the invention of the catheter, opened a clinic at Harvard, and created a project for the government." He points to a brand new IPod speaker system on top of his television—"My son bought this for me. It's for me to listen to music." I love the old soul, new technology. "Harvey has two children, and Renee has three children. From one of Renee's children, we have two great grandchildren." I hope I live to see *my* great grandchildren.

The tone turns again when we talk about values and lessons. "It was always important for me to support my family," Samson says with solidity and purpose. "I worked hard all my life." He explains how deeply he wanted his children to get a proper education and how happy he was to send both of them to the University of Pennsylvania (my alma mater). "During World War Two, I sometimes worked [several] jobs a day. From ten o'clock to four thirty I worked at the Ward. Some days, I'd work the twelve o'clock shift somewhere else, and then I'd work for the U.S. Mint printing purple hearts and money. Necessity is the mother of invention." What a great phrase—it has never lost it's relevance.

After Dorothy died, Samson found a new companion named Yetta. He was married to her for eleven years until she died of diabetes. Both of his marriages were good ones.

As we speak, Ann drives into the room on her electric wheelchair. She seems hesitant to enter, but her fast-moving wheelchair keeps her from turning back. "I hope I'm not interrupting anything," she says quietly. Samson turns around slowly. "Oh no, it's ok. This young lady is taking down my history and she's sending me the bill." We all chuckle.

"Sam, are you sure you don't mind if I borrow it?" I don't know what she's talking about, until he makes a three point turn with his wheelchair and opens the bottom drawer of his dresser, revealing a talis bag. "It's for my bas mitzvah," Ann says proudly, her voice louder than before. "It's on Saturday." How exciting it is to see this—Samson is letting this woman, presumably in her sixties, borrow his talis so that she may wear it during her unconventionally late rite of passage. A cheerful rabbinic intern at the Center named Shula enters the room and helps Ann say a prayer as she wraps herself in the talis. I watch as ancient landscapes of blue, green, red, and purple threads envelop her. "It's beautiful, just beautiful," she repeats over and over. "Are you sure you want me to have this?" Samson looks at her and pauses for a moment, and suddenly he jokes: "If I offered it to you, don't you think I want you to have it?" He looks at me and smiles. I am starting to understand his chilly warmth as sarcasm, not as means to offend.

Samson says he has learned many important lessons in his lifetime and makes note of a few: "It's important to be honest, not to do drugs or smoke, and never to gamble (except in Atlantic City, sometimes). You must get an education, try to be aggressive, don't beat your wife up, be congenial, applicable, never go to bed angry—always have an agreeable marriage, teach your children proper things, and use authority when you need to." Fine words from a fine man. Before I leave, I bend down to shake his hand and cups my hand in his. "It was lovely meeting you," I say as I kiss his cheek, and from that, he uncovers a smile with much expression.

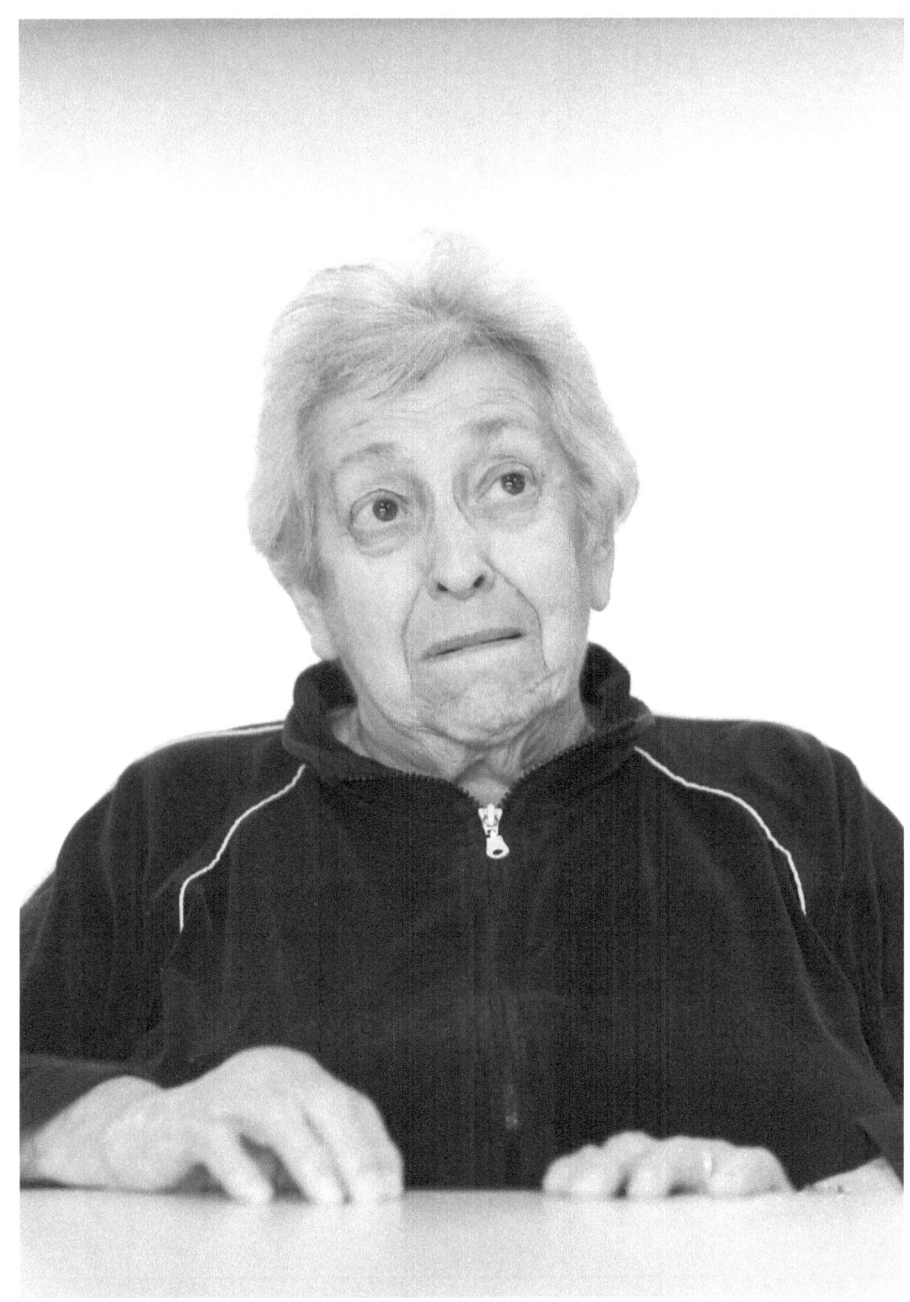

SYLVIA FORD
Age: 83

"I've created a name for myself," Sylvia says, tapping on the table in the hallway of her residential floor. "PITA". She smiles and raises her eyebrows.

"'Pain In The Ass.'"

Though this line comes at the end of our interview, it deserves to be mentioned in the beginning, as this defines Sylvia Ford—outspoken, bold, and without excuses.

"I was born in Philadelphia, Pennsylvania on July 7th, 1926. At the age of two, my father came here from Russia. [In his adult years] he was a bandleader and a great entertainer." From what I've heard about Sylvia prior to our interview, it seems like she is an entertainer herself. "My mother was born in Philadelphia." She says. I ask Sylvia what her mother was like, and her face softens. "My mother was a gracious, sweet, loving companion to my father, a loving daughter, and the glue of the entire family." Sylvia smiles at the thought of her parents and refers to them constantly during the interview—exactly what I would do if I were being interviewed. "My mother had a fabulous sense of humor." I'm not surprised—Sylvia has to have gotten that from someone.

She continues on about her family: "I'm one of four daughters, and we grew up in a loving and caring family. We lived at 62nd and Spruce, and during the Depression, my grandparents got older and couldn't live alone. It was hard for them to move around, so my parents and my grandparents joined forces and we lived together on 60th and Christian in a four-bedroom house." Talk about a full house! I can just picture a group of vibrant, active daughters swirling around their older parents and grandparents. It reminds of *Little Women*—a book that happens to be Sylvia's favorite.

Sylvia tells me about her childhood: "I was very bright, I went to William Cullen Bryant School until eighth grade, then to Shaw Junior High for one year, and then West Philadelphia High. In tenth grade, I had to take typing because my sister needed my help." I imagine that Sylvia is a devoted sibling. "What was your relationship with your siblings like?" I ask. She lets out a dramatic sigh. "Well, I'm number two of four—we're all very close. One lives in Ambler, one in New York, one in Jersey. We love each other, respect each other—two are rich and two are not! My baby sister has four children, ten grandchildren, and my older sister had two daughters, and numerous grandchildren and great grandchildren."

I'm curious if Sylvia ever faced any notable challenges in her life—I imagine that living with so many sisters would cause tension. But once again, Sylvia surprises me with a very emphatic "No". She doesn't seem to let anything bother her—the eternal optimist. Sylvia recalls summers she spent in Poland, Maine with her family. Her father ran a hotel there, and she can picture herself playing on the slide, gliding in the waters of Lake Tripp. I went to Tripp Lake Camp, an all-girls overnight camp on that same lake for eight summers. We laugh at the amazing coincidence. "I loved it there," she says. So did I.

Sylvia is sure to tell me that she wasn't a young girl interested in clothes or make-up. "I was a tomboy," she says with pride. "I liked boys better than girls, they were more fun to be with." Her honesty makes me laugh. "In our day, we used to have skates made out of orange crates—when I was about twelve, some of the guys had a lemonade stand and I gave them lemons [in turn] for a bike and they taught me how to ride." Her experiences with boys as a young girl were an omen for her later life—she birthed three sons, two of whom have their own two sons. Tomboy or not, Sylvia is a lady among men.

She is a real game player, too. But not the manipulative kind—the board and yard game kind. "I played 'Red Rover Red Rover' on the side streets—my father didn't let us ride bikes, so we rollerskated. I remember we always played "School", we had backyards in those days, yards with metal fences with a back alley, and my father's brother and his family lived next door to us in a loving neighborhood. At home, we played lots of games like Monopoly and cards—I know four different games of Solitaire—and in the living room we would always have a puzzle. Everyone could put in a piece when they walked by."

I ask Sylvia what kinds of jobs she held. She has quite a list. "As a child, I was always a babysitter. I made good money—about a dollar an hour! Then I worked for A.S. Beck Shoe Company in Camden, and when I graduated from High School, I was a clerk typist. After I had my children, I worked at Chase Savings and Loan. When my husband passed away, I went to work in the school system, and I became a non-teaching assistant, and I worked part-time and typed for a lawyer, and then I worked at that job until I was seventy, and then I worked part-time again after that." Being eighty-three,

Sylvia only stopped working recently. She doesn't waste a minute of her life. It's inspiring.

In her long-winded list of jobs, mention of her husband's passing gets my wheels turning, and I ask how they met. Sylvia lets out a low-toned chuckle and rolls back and forth in her wheelchair—as if she is dancing. "I met my husband at my friend's wedding. My father played at her wedding, and she arranged for [Sydney, my future husband] to take me. He had a girlfriend at the time, but the list was limited so she asked him to be my so-called 'date'." It's like a movie. "After six months, we were married in March 1948. It was fun. He was in the real estate business and was a very nice man. He was religious, and I agreed to keep a Jewish house." Like Sydney, Sylvia was brought up with a proud Jewish identity. Her family went to Hebrew Sunday School at the West Philadelphia Jewish Community Center. Among the other things they had in common, Sydney also came from a large family. "He was one of six children," she explains. "The nearest one in age to him was six years older. The other ones were all out of the house when he was growing up. He was the baby." Sylvia pauses. "He died first of his siblings. We were married sixteen years."

Eager to make Sylvia feel better, I prompt her with something that I am sure brings her joy—her sons. "My oldest son Louis was born in '49, the next Joseph was born in '56, and the youngest S. Phillip was born in '58. Louis is an accountant and controller for a small company. My middle son is deceased—he got into the drug scene and got caught, my baby is fifty and lives in Colorado—right now he's on disability, and he used to work on a campus for fraternities as a Greek Life advisor." Her kids help to create the eclectic collage of Sylvia's life story. She loves her kids, and in that soft moment she reveals a sensitive story: "My son goes by S. Phillip Ford because hates his name. He was only five years old when his father died, and soon after I dated a guy with his name, 'Sam', and he hated him." I can only imagine the traumatizing feeling of losing a father at that age and the discomfort of sharing a name with someone who carries such a heavy reality.

I ask Sylvia about her lessons and values and she lays them out like cards on a table. "Education is always important. It is important to always play honest and fair, never lie, never steal, and always respect the people you know."

"Sometimes people hold back and don't tell the truth. But, you know what? I say 'Fuck it'. I've spent my whole life doing what other people wanted—I was a good wife, a devoted daughter, and I'm a loving mother, but now it's time for me to do what I want."

Sylvia is the quintessential example of "What you see is what you get", and like the neon blue of the nylon sweatsuit she wears, it is refreshing.

GERTRUDE STEIN
Age: 95

After many days of poking my head into Gertrude's empty room, I finally ask a nurse where I can find her.

"See over there? She's the one in the salmon colored sweater with the beaded necklace."

I stare into the small sea of women gathered around the communal television in the "living room" and catch sight of her just beyond them, the back of her wheelchair facing me. I can see that she's chatting with Shirley, one of the Center's social workers, so I don't want to interrupt, but as soon as I approach them, Shirley stands up and smiles. "It's okay, you're welcome to sit and talk to her." I look down and see a Pumpernick's menu in Shirley's hand. "We're having lunch together today, so I can just meet with her later." Gertrude dictates her order—a turkey sandwich, not too many bells and whistles—and Shirley is on her way. "I'm simple," Gertrude says matter-of-factly. Simplicity is the theme of our interview.

Gertrude is a beautiful woman. Her hair is a soft red, her eyes are green and wide, and her thin, rose-colored mouth is the outlet through which her sharp wit is exposed. As I sit down, I explain to Gertrude why I'm here and what I'm doing. "I'm interviewing different residents," I begin. She interrupts me: "Mmhm. So what are you going to do with them? Put them on a computer and then erase them later?" I explain to her that I'm writing a book to be published, and she likes the idea. "Well, I'm not telling you any secrets, but we can talk."

Gertrude begins by telling me about her family: "We were very poor, I can tell you that. But in spite of that, my brothers and my sisters turned out well. My brother Joe is ninety-seven and he calls me every night at nine o'clock. EVERY NIGHT and we talk for maybe fifteen, twenty minutes—I don't know what we talk about! He remembers everything—he was in the Second World War. He is in a very successful business—he's in paper, and he's been to Cuba and all over the world. Whoever he meets, he remembers." This is the first suggestion of Gertrude's pride in her family, and delicate moments like these pop up throughout the interview.

"As a family, we grew up in the Depression," she continues. "Times were different. Back then, you could get coffee for a nickel." It is the timeless statement that brings to life how different the world is today.

I open my mouth to ask another question, but a nurse who is thrilled to see Gertrude interrupts me. "Hiiiiiiii!" she sings, her voice spiced with a Caribbean accent. She stops for a short conversation and keeps walking down the hall. "The staff here are *very* nice," Gertrude tells me.

I ask about her parents, and her answers are simple: "My father was a tailor, and his family was very good to us—they came to America in 1910. He had four sisters and one brother and they took us in all our lives, and they were really the only family that we had. My mother, I don't really remember what family she had, but she did have some sisters and brothers. My mother was from Poland. But my father's family was really good to us—we used to have holiday dinners together. It was very nice." Positivity is the name of the game with Gertrude—she does not nor does she ever seem to have sweated the small stuff.

I ask her about the jobs she held when she was young. "I worked for an advertising company," she tells me. "Well, actually, they were engravers. We worked on Walnut Street." I can picture Gertrude power-walking through a younger city of Philadelphia, stunning and determined. "My first job was ten dollars a week, and I paid my mother five dollars and I kept the other five dollars and used it to buy clothes. I was a bridesmaid in one of my friend's weddings, and I bought a dress at—what is it called—Lerner's, yes—and bought the dress for eight dollars! This blue gown—and the wedding was on Broad and Girard Streets. But that's the way things were—it was different! You don't have things like that today. Now, an orange is a dollar and a banana is fifty-nine cents. When we bought an orange it was five to ten cents—we would get a bunch of bananas for fifteen cents." Gertrude pauses. "Later on, I worked for the Philadelphia Geriatric Center for twenty-five years and served as the Secretary of Social Service. I loved it." After our interview, I bump into Shirley who was planning lunch with Gertrude. She raves about her, and she tells me that Gertrude won the Citizenship Award at the Center for being an outstanding resident.

"When did you meet your husband?" I ask. Gertrude lets a puff of laughter exit her lips—the first one of the day. "I was twenty years old when I met Martin. I was allergic to Poison Ivy and I was invited to a picnic with my cousin—also named Gertrude!—and we got in some and I broke out in hives. It was so bad that I had to stay home the next day. Well, Martin was visiting a friend who lived across the street from me at the time, and we met." I can picture Gertrude making an amazing impression on him—even with her body swollen from itchy red blotches. When I ask about her wedding, Gertrude maintains her straightforwardness. "I had a very small wedding—it was the Depression—and we went to the rabbi's house, and then back to our house. We went on a three-day honeymoon to New York. It was very nice." Everything is "nice".

I ask about her children but before she can open her mouth, another nurse walks by and greets Gertrude with a warm, bellowing "Hi Darlin'!" Gertrude has a fan-base.

I wish that Gertrude will open up more, but I build so much respect for her privacy that I decide not to pry. When she said "no secrets" she meant "not too many details"—except when it comes to her children. Hearing her talk about them is like opening the lid of a music box.

"My daughter Arlene and my son Jerry are wonderful and have given me five wonderful grandchildren in all. Arlene's kids—Ellen, Allison, and David went to Harvard, Yale and Penn. Very smart kids. David went to school in Beijing and was there during the uprising. He got punched in the jaw!" We laugh together, and I jump on the opportunity to hear more about the injury. Not to my surprise, Gertrude is a woman of habit and leaves it there. "That's all I know about it," she says. "He's very handsome and very bright. Jerry's son Andrew is in medical school paying off the years he owes the army at a hospital. At the Center, we make bags and I made Andrew a bag, of course with his name, Dr. Andrew Stein, and put in implements—a thermometer and other things—and he loved it! I know he got my package because he called me twice and he knows that I love him and wish him the best. I'm very proud of him. Dara, Jerry's daughter, graduated from college and is a teacher and I'm very proud of her, too."

I ask Gertrude about the role of Judaism in her life. "Judaism has always been very important to me—I went to Hebrew school and I was confirmed. My kids were bar and bas mitzvah'ed. My mother was always kosher. When I first got married I was kosher but then I stopped being strictly kosher. We had a kosher home—a few infractions! The kids know they're Jewish—I think it's still a very important part of their lives."

I'm about to ask her to elaborate but another nurse stops to chat. At this point, I am sure we will never get through our interview, but I laugh because I feel like I'm sitting with the Queen of England. "You're loved around here," I say. In true Gertrude fashion, she shrugs her shoulders. "I like [the nurses]. They're very nice. We have a knitting club here and I teach lots of the girls from Haiti how to make scarves, hats, and blankets. They've never had that kind of activity, and I like doing it. We even donated 300 hats to CHOP and Hadassah from the knitting club."

Gertrude manages to make a difference to everyone around her and takes no credit for any of it. I ask her what has brought her the greatest sense of accomplishment, and I am warmed by her answer.

"My grandchildren's happiness makes me happy—when they call, just their attitudes, their happiness—it feels good to feel secure. They have given me the greatest sense of accomplishment."

I turn the tape recorder over and realize it has been off the entire time. Luckily I have been scribbling down notes, but instead of getting upset about it, I try to think like Gertrude and not sweat the small stuff.

"Do you have any other questions for me?" Gertrude has places to go.

"No, that's all I have. Thank you so much for meeting with me."

"What days are you here?" She asks.

"Tuesdays and Wednesdays," I tell her.

"Come by and say hello," she says and with that, she pushes herself off in the opposite direction, disappearing around a corner.

HERMAN DREYFUSS
Age: 91½

Herman is a hard man to pin down. I came to his room three times to interview him, and he was never available—his schedule was constantly packed with appointments, meetings, and other engagements. "Now is not a good time," he said as I stood in his doorway, his feet tiptoeing slowly as he pushed his walker forward. His voice was remarkably high and quiet while still maintaining a noticeably European accent. "I have many things to tend to today." The borders of this apartment were lined with stunning watercolor paintings encased in frames. The Staff told me that Herman was an artist, and I was eager to discuss his work with him. I hoped he would one day make some time for me, and finally, after three weeks, I was able to set up an appointment.

"You've come highly recommended, you know," I say, sitting down in the chair next to his bedside table. He smiles. "Oh yes?" he says, almost whispering. "W-who sent you here?" I explain. He sits down on the edge of his bed, hesitant at first. "What do you want to know?" And from there we begin—slowly but surely.

"I was born in Krakow, Poland in 1918 and came to America in March 1938 with nothing. I had to meet people myself, I had to make a living, and I couldn't go to school because I hadn't finished my degree. I had no means." When I ask Herman to elaborate, he seems uncertain. I am patient until he is willing to speak further. "When I was in Europe, I went to the University of Vienna. I received an education for two years but left right before the war and couldn't finish."

He travels back from America to Europe in his mind and describes more of his experiences as a young man there. "I was an only child. My relationship with my parents was strained at times but they were my parents so that was that. I spoke many languages—French, Polish, and German. I always did teaching, and I went to Paris many times. There, I joined a colony and became an interpreter to the head of police." I am impressed with everything Herman says—I can picture him as a young dynamic man cultured by his travels. Herman shrugs his curved shoulders and makes a modest comment: "I did not think of myself as anything special. I did what I had to do."

When I ask Herman what it was like to be a young Jew during wartime, he pauses to ponder the question. "I was not proud to be a Jew, then. Anti-Semitism in Vienna was not a nice thing." I could tell he was holding back. "I do not want to talk if we're going to talk about the war," he says, emphatic even with a hushed tone. I suggest another route of conversation. "There are other important things we can talk about. We'll stick with those." He seems happier with this idea, so we move on.

Herman exposes a wide, nearly toothless grin when I ask about his wife. "My wife was beautiful and quiet," he says. "Her name was Sylvia Rosner. Her parents came from Austria. We were married at the beginning of the war." With Sylvia, Herman had three children—two daughters Corinne and Shelly, and one son Jerome who passed away. Herman grows visibly sad, so I do not ask any more questions about Jerome.

"What was your life like in America?" I ask, hoping to veer off into a completely different direction. Herman takes long pauses throughout the entire interview, but they are well worth it. His stories are wonderful.

"The people who sponsored me to come to America wanted me to get a job so they could, you know, get me off their hands. I worked in clothing factories while my wife worked by typing. I later resided with my uncle in West Philadelphia. When I arrived, I wrote a twenty-page essay entitled 'Why I Love The U.S.' to Eleanor Roosevelt. She responded and thanked me for the letter! She said it was very nice." I am not sure if Herman would have stayed in Poland if he hadn't felt the urgency to leave during the war. What is clear is Herman's appreciation for the opportunities available to him living in America and the people he was able to meet. "I would meet in the afternoons with Hans Heinz, a West Philadelphia High School teacher. We would meet downtown at the Art Alliance and talk about Franz Werfel and Gustav Mahler."

As I scribble notes in my book, I know this is an ideal segway by which to discuss his artwork. "I've heard you are an incredible artist," I say to him. He exposes another priceless grin. "I wouldn't say that," he shrugs, but as soon as I ask to see his work, he pushes himself off his bed as fast as he can and layers my lap with the paintings that lined the floor. Every piece is more striking than the next: delicate washes of paint dotted with sailboats inspired by his time in New England, landscapes of similar towns peppered with buildings, lighthouses, and trees. Herman also works more abstractly: organic lines of black ink filled in with vibrant liquid colors creating shapes and textures only he truly understands. I am in awe of his talent. "I paint everyday," he tells me.

Herman stands over me, holding my hand as I peer into his sketchbooks, the pages stiff from dried paint. "There are so many that I have, these are only a few," he says, watching the pages as they turn. I reach the last few pages of the first of two books he has given me and stop to read them.

Herman has penciled messages of self-affirmation, interspersed with small drawings of trees. "*I am strong. My family loves me. I am capable. I am not alone. I will be fine.*"

"What are these?" I ask. "They helped me," he admits. "I was in the hospital, and they were ways for me to express myself." Herman, already gentle when I first met him, reaches an unprecedented delicacy. But at the same time, he shows himself the strongest I have seen him. His willingness to open up and give himself to his emotions provides incredible richness to his work.

As I look over to his windowsill arranged with pictures, I notice framed photographs of two young boys. "Those are my grandsons," Herman says, the sadness dissolving from his gaze. He points to the younger boy with a mop top of blonde hair. "He is Ian." Herman makes his way to his dresser, slips out a manila folder, and opens it to reveal a piece of artwork layered with paint, paper, and ink, much like his own. The bottom right corner is marked with Ian's name. "He takes classes. He loves art."

Herman tells me that showing his art and celebrating his children give him the greatest sense of accomplishment.

As I return to another sketchbook, the first ten or so pages are filled with different versions of the same familiar scene. "Is this the view from your apartment window?" I ask him. We both look out the window. His drawings are accurate but very much consistent with his style: he outlines the wood dividing the windowpanes with pen and blends ink and watercolor to make out the landscape set beyond it. "Yes," he says. He points beyond the glass to the trees, the grass, and the parking lot. "I stare out here everyday," he says. Herman sometimes wishes he were sitting somewhere else painting the scenery of a vast countryside, but he makes the most of his view and uses his imagination to create nuance and variation. The sun is strong today and glows on Herman's face. "To be free, that is art."

MILTON SWIREN
Age: 89

Within moments of entering his apartment, I learn that Milt is an incredible pianist. He tells me he learned to play by ear, and he can play anything after he hears the first few notes just one or two times.

"I've been known to tickle the keys," he says, chuckling.

Milt does not even know me yet, but I am quickly privileged to a private concert. He hands me a spiral notebook. "Here, pick whatever songs you like, and I'll play whatever you want. I supposedly know all of these songs." I open the book, and there they are: at least fifty songs, all hand-alphabetized and labeled with the first few musical notes of each song. Milt is very organized. I do not hesitate to take him up on the offer, as I see many songs I know, love, and have not heard in a long while. I already can feel the green of envy swimming through my veins—I played piano just the way he did for eleven years but haven't touched it for nearly a decade. Milt inspires me to reconsider.

Milt's fingers slide across the two rows of ivory keys as he plays "Hatikvah", "The Hills are Alive" from *The Sound of Music*, "Embraceable You" (one of my parents' favorite songs), "Memories" from *Cats* (the first song I ever learned on the piano), and "I Dreamed a Dream" from *Les Miserables*, a song he tells me he learned from *Britain's Got Talent's* biggest hit, Susan Boyle. His beautiful mahogany Electone piano, located next to his Kitchenette in the corner of the living room, plays like an organ and is decorated with primary-colored switches, all with some marvelous musical purpose. The last thing I want to do is tear him away from the piano, but I ask if we can speak for a little while so long as he plays for me afterwards. He smiles one of one hundred times during the interview, makes himself comfortable in his armchair, and we begin.

"I was born in 1919. In other words, I'm gonna be—oh this is really great. See, this memory comes and goes—I'll be ninety years old this November." When I tell him he doesn't look ninety (he really does not), he jokes: "I've been accused of it!"

"I was born in Wilmington, Delaware," Milt continues, "and my father was a rabbi and he spent most of his time in Philadelphia." Milt pauses after I ask him about his relationship with his father. "Well," he begins, "he was so busy that I didn't see much of him—he had a congregation and was very nice, and truly busy from one to the other. But he was truly the work of the saying: 'The people come first'. But he was my father and that was it." I assume that his father's status in the Jewish community influenced the role of Judaism in his life. It did, but not in the way I think it would. As Milt explains, the rebel effect took hold. "Judaism wasn't really an important part of my childhood—my older brother, younger brother and me didn't care for it, but my sister liked it. Orthodox was too much for us, and my father was very nice to us, even though he was disappointed because he wanted to have at least one son who would carry on the tradition."

Milt is touchingly honest when I ask about his mother. "My mother had cancer and she died relatively young so I didn't have enough of her. I missed her terribly. I imagine I was a little older than a teenager when she passed away—and they didn't know much in those days [about how to treat cancer] so it hit me like a ton of bricks. In fact, it stunned me, but she was my mother and I loved her and that was the nice part of it." When I ask to hear more about his mother, he perks up. "She was a sweet person to everyone—she was a rabbi's wife and there was a big load on her shoulders but she was always graceful." His description reminds me of my mom. I can feel the love he has for her, and the pain he still feels almost seven decades later.

Milt expands on his siblings: "My older brother sort of took charge of things and he did a good job for my younger brother and me. If someone needed money, he took care of the situation. He went to World War Two and later I went to World War Two and we both ended up in England and then he came to see me. Everything was secret, and two days later it was D Day and my brother went across to France and then I didn't see him for quite a while. My outfit stayed in England and then we went to France and we had all sorts of adventures, our train went off the tracks—it was done deliberately—some of the French people were nice to us but some of them weren't. So after four years, three months, and two days, I came home. It was amazing to come home, I was so happy. A lot of guys were happy—that was the highlight. My sister was home when I got home. She tried to be mother to everybody and she was Orthodox, but we made things go right."

After he got home, Milt got married. He is such a kind man, and I anticipate a beautiful love story. "I got married—I don't remember the year, already. When I came home from the war, a friend of mine was a real 'wow' to the women, I approached him and said 'You know a million women, you introduce me to just *one* of them'. So what happened was that my friend supposedly introduced me to a young lady by accident but it ended up being the right one—it was the one I was looking for. So, sure enough, I ended up marrying her—her name was Bernice." Milt looks out of the large window that faces his chair, and his eyes glitter in the sun. "She was very sweet, very nice. We had a real flamboyant wedding, it was quite the situation—every kind of imaginable nice decoration—it was a real razzmatazz—a real highlight." He shows me their wedding portraits. They look like movie stars.

Milt cannot remember exactly how many years he and Bernice were married, but he says it was for a 'long time'. When I ask what happened to her, he reveals a story that he says shook him deeply. "Her esophagus went blooey and what they wanted to do was to put in some kind of artificial thing, and she sounded like a fog horn—a horrible sound. And she had gone to the doctor before that and said 'If anything such and such happens, I want to end it'. So I signed [a living will for her] and she signed the thing and we never thought for a moment we would have to use it. But things got worse, and she didn't want to live like that. There was no quality of life and that was a horrible time of my life." On the lip of his piano is a series of pictures—each of them of him with the same woman—a different woman than Bernice. I recognize the woman from the Center—she lives one floor above him. I decide to wait to ask Milt about her later.

"Do you have kids?" I ask. "Yes, I have one son, Bruce, named after Bernice—he's six feet four inches!" Milt laughs as he stands up to grab a picture of Bruce. With his beard, Bruce could be the grandson of Paul Bunyan. "He calls me everyday," Milt says. "He lives in New York, and he comes here about every week or two and we go places where they have Jewish food." It turns out that Milt and I share the same favorite delicatessen, and we go off on a tangent about cabbage soup and the like. Milt likes how the restaurant never seems to change.

"Anyhow," Milt continues, "Bruce was married twice—the first marriage was to a women's lib feminist so that didn't work, and the second marriage is to a woman who is very short! They both work for the government, so it's like hush-hush work. They're both very bright. He's happy, so I keep my nose out of it."

Talk of government brings us to Milt's vocational past. Milt began as a teacher of science—"Astronomy, this, that, and the other thing" he says—at Fels Junior High School. "I was sort of known for making my own things that would help keep the students interested in science," he says. "I made posters and put them around—it helped somewhat but they were an entirely different kind of people coming into the school, and none [of my fellow teachers] could stand it. It got to be bad when they did snuff. I could have stayed for a few more years, but it wasn't very pleasant. I would come in in the morning, and there would be dirty stuff on the floor—it was no place for a Jewish boy!"

Suddenly the conversation turns to the view outside of his apartment. Days before, Lilly showed me her own garden in the backyard of the Inn, and next to her's was Milt's garden—lush rows of beet red and deep green plants. He is thrilled that I have heard of his garden. "My favorite thing is to get up in the morning, put up the blinds, and have something lovely to look at." It is such a pleasant day, and I am so happy Milt finds joy in his view.

It's time to ask about the pictures on his piano. "So—tell me about Sylvia."

"Sylvia. Sylvia says that when I got [to the Center]—I can't remember how long ago that was, a few years—that I was in a coma, in a wheelchair, and I wouldn't talk to anyone. When my wife died, I wasn't myself for a long time, and frankly looking back I don't remember what happened to me. But Sylvia said, and I don't remember this, that after a while I would only let her push me around in my wheelchair. I was attracted to her, and after a while I got better. She was the reason I got my life back." It's hard to bounce back after a severe loss, and Milt proves that it is possible. "We like spending time together, laughing, it's really great. She is so sweet." I look over at a picture of the two of them on Halloween; he's wearing the thick black glasses and fake nose, and Sylvia's wearing a bright pink beehive wig and neon green glasses over her real ones. "There is no deadline on finding a companion," I say. "You're absolutely right. That is so true."

Milt returns to the piano to play me "I Love You For Sentimental Reasons", another song that reminds me of my parents. I ask him to play the "Jeopardy" theme song, and he furrows his brow before playing it perfectly. He really *can* play anything.

"See if you can stump me!" he says. I flip through the book and find one. "Let Me Call You Sweetheart," I suggest. It sounds like a carousel has entered the room, spinning with sweet harmonies and playful chords.

I tell Milt I would like to come back to hear him play again, and he smiles. "I would love that. You can come back whenever you like, and if you ever need anything, please let me know." I give him a hug, and he kisses my cheek. "You made my day," he says. "You made mine, too."

EUGENE WINSTON
Age: 91½

At twelve o'clock on my first day at the Center, I walked into Mustard & Rye, the half-restaurant, half-cafeteria for some lunch. I approached the display of deli sandwiches and salads and stood next to an older man with a walker picking out his lunch from the shelves. As I effortlessly grabbed a turkey sandwich, the man next to me was having a little trouble, so I asked him if he desired any assistance. He looked at me from under a black baseball cap, the name "Pop-Pop" embroidered in bold white letters on the front, and mumbled "Yes" under his breath. He instructed me to his choosing—a whitefish platter with egg, cucumber, and tomato, a bagel, and a small cup of regular coffee with skim milk and one sugar. As I brought his tray back to the table of his choosing, he asked me if I would like to sit with him.

Gene became my first friend.

From that day forward, Gene and I have eaten lunch every Tuesday and Wednesday afternoon at twelve o'clock, and it is the highlight of both his and my week. It is the same routine—he sits at our table while I pick out his lunch (whitefish or herring, depending on his mood), gather his utensils, and sit back down with him, assembling his bagels and placing a napkin on his lap to keep clean. He asks me about my project, I ask him about the stock market (he follows it closely), and we enjoy each other's company for an hour until I go back to work.

Today it is different. Today, after our hour together, we walk back toward his room and situate ourselves in a little nook off of the hallway. It is Gene's turn to be interviewed.

"I was born in Williamsburg, Brooklyn, New York. I came from a big family—I'm the youngest of seven—two sisters and five brothers. But then again, they always had big families in Europe." Gene has taken off his Pop-Pop hat to reveal his gray hair. I think about his siblings and how he might be the only one still alive. Not just alive, but full of life. I wonder how it might feel to be the last left of seven. "My parents were from Lithuania," he continues. Gene remembers his fathers name—Sam—but can't remember his mother's. He looks off down the hall and makes a face he has made so many times before—one of frustration. I ask him to tell me more about his parents, and he is happy to be back on track.

"They were hard working Jewish people. My father always struggled to make a living, y'know he had seven children, and my mother was also very helpful in the store." Gene tells me that his parents sold fruit and vegetables in their own shop. "What were your siblings like?" I ask. Gene brightens. "The next one to me was Phil and he was ten years older. He and all of my older siblings were born in Europe, I was the only one born in America." I picture Gene, a little infant, the American apple of his family's European eyes. Gene runs off the list of his siblings. "I had a sister Leah, a brother Al, a brother Irving, and another brother Ben." His face revealed the same frustrated look as he searches his memory for his sixth sibling's name, his sister, but yields nothing.

"What was your childhood like?" I ask. Gene's face brightens again. "I was a lucky child! I had a big family and they all loved me and they were so proud of me. They took good care of me and they took their turns taking care of me!" When I ask Gene about the games he used to play as a kid, he delivers a very pragmatic response: "Poor kids did what they could."

I ask Gene what distinct memories he has of his childhood. "I have a lot of beautiful memories—my siblings and I always had a good time together and they gave me everything I needed. My parents didn't have much, so they supplemented the things I didn't have. We used to ride with my parents on horse and wagon and took orders for the store—they had to keep me someplace since there was no one who could stay home with me." Gene's warm stare gives me a true sense of the happiness he felt in the care of his siblings. I feel the same way when I am with mine.

Gene grew up Orthodox but does not practice religion the way he once did. "I went to kheder," he says. When I ask him what subjects he enjoyed learning, I am not surprised to receive another simple answer: "Whatever they taught me, I had to learn." Gene faced everything in his life as a job at which he was determined to succeed. As we sit together, he still has the same youthful, unwavering spirit.

Many weeks before, some of the Staff informed me that Gene was an accountant, so I ask him about it. "My brother Irving became an accountant—he took the right courses to get to where he needed to be, and he looked after me and told me what I had to learn, and I learned it all pretty well. He was a pretty strict teacher—a good teacher—and he took me in with him, and we roped my son in, and then I took the [accounting business] over myself. Irving left to go into the automobile business and he didn't want to fool with cheap accounting work anymore so I built a pretty good practice. I didn't need other people looking after me, so I was happy not to have that expense." Gene speaks proudly about his business sense: "I made a pretty good living, and had a good understanding of everything, and took care of my clients when they called. They loved me and I loved them and I made a lot of money from them." I can see so much of my own Zayda in Gene—his aptitude, drive, and resolve.

I change the subject to his romantic past. The first day we sat down to lunch, I found out that Gene was separated from his wife. I bring the subject up with him again, and he sheds light on their relationship. "I met my wife in high school. We went to the same school—we fooled around together and then when I came home from the war, I married her. I don't remember her name—she's in another nursing home around here. What the heck was her name? Oh well, I didn't use her name so often. I have it written down somewhere." I ask him what she was like. "She was a nice lady but I kept going forward, you know, in life, with what I did and I couldn't take her with me. She was backward—many times I got very busy at work and it was really two different worlds, and she couldn't get used to my work and I couldn't remain backwards. So we didn't get along too well. My son brought her [to a nursing facility] first, and then I came later when I wasn't doing well. She went her way, and I went mine." Again, simplicity.

Gene always talks about his son when we eat together, and I am eager to learn more about him. "My son's name is Ira. He's gonna be fifty, I guess. He's the greatest boy I ever had." Gene pauses and laughs. "He's the *only* one I ever had! But really, I had him under my wing and I made him take the kind of stuff that was going to be useful and he did excellent in high school. Then he came to the University of Pennsylvania and was a star student all the way through and when he graduated he took a job with the University helping one of his professors. Ira worked with him in the summer and off-seasons and then the professor took him in permanently and Ira became an assistant professor. He had talent, and I steered him the right way." Gene adores his son and is comforted by their close relationship. "He visits me at least once a week here. He has two sons—Robert, who's older and is running in our field, and Andrew who's younger, he's the real sharp, bright one." Gene tells me he'll show me pictures of them when we walk back to his room from our table in the hallway.

Gene is a man of values. "I've always taught my kids to be honest, and do clear, clean work to make everybody proud of you. The most important thing you can teach is to do good work, because if you can't do good work, you can't amount to anything. I don't care *who* your father or grandfather is, it's still the most important thing." I ask if Gene was taught those same lessons as a child, and he is quick to tell me "No". "I wasn't taught the same lessons. I grew up with six brothers and sisters and I learned how to be a family member, whatever they wanted to teach me, I learned. I took good care of my kids because they were the only ones, not like me who had six others. It was different times—I made lots of money so they got what they needed, and they deserved it. They still do."

"What do you do with your time now?" I inquire, knowing full well what he does but asking nonetheless. "Now I try to learn what's around me, what my whereabouts are, and I guess I stuck with the arts and service and things like that. I'm not as religious as I should be, but I've been through it all, I know it all." I ask Gene if he has any interest in a further pursuit of Judaism. "I'm not sure if I want to be more religious—this is not a religious world. You have to learn to make a living before you do anything else, without money you don't have much. I learned the value of money pretty quickly. I would do simple things and collect a lot of money—whatever it is I did and I was successful and it paid off in many ways." Gene returns to the initial question. "I'm trying to keep up on my studies even though my capabilities have changed." Gene doesn't give up on the things he cares about. He keeps himself busy with one of his favorite pastimes, the stock market.

"How are your stocks doing?" I ask. "My stocks?" Gene chuckles. "They do what I tell them! I'm glad to see that in the last few weeks there's been a vast improvement. Stocks is a business of it's own—you have to know when to buy them, when to sell them and trade them, and you have to be familiar with them and be one step in front of everyone else. I've learned how to be in touch with everything. I'm a pretty good stock handler."

From what I hear, Gene certainly is. He is the resident stock expert and spends every day with his head buried in the stock pages of the newspapers. Gene used to inquire for his own stock lists off the Internet, but now volunteers print them out and deliver them to him.

"My son has benefited well from all of my stocks," Gene explains. "He takes care of a lot of them now and we go back and forth—what to sell, what to buy. And when you buy 'em cheap, you can always make money. That's been my habit, buying some cheap stocks and they turn into the best stocks, and then you have merchandise to sell or keep or do whatever you want to do. It's an art, it's a profession."

Watching Gene talk about stocks is a beautiful thing. He has become like a grandfather to me, and it is thrilling to see a man of his age engaged and dedicated to something so ever changing and unpredictable. "I must have, between me and my son, over 100 stocks, so it's a big business. Some you have to look at day-to-day, and others you can put aside and let them grow and benefit from them, and those you have to be careful with so you can fall back on them if you need to. It's good to be invested in lots of different things—I have a good eye for things that are going to grow and things that will be good on investments." I ask Gene if his stocks have become a part of his relationship with other people. I can picture Gene spending time with fellow residents or older volunteers helping them with their portfolios. "I can only do this stuff on my own," he tells me, "though I did try to help a few people." Gene says that when he tries to help, most of the time people don't do it the way he would like them to. He can only lead them to the stream, but he can't make them drink. Nonetheless, Gene is still open to giving guidance. "They always have me to fall back on if they need help."

Gene gathers his stock papers from the table and tucks them into the basket on his walker as we head toward his room. The walls are covered with pictures of Gene as a younger man, his face fuller, his smile wider. Gene sits in his chair beside his bed, and I give myself a tour, looking at pictures of Ira, Robert, and Andrew—each of their faces similar to Gene's. Beside his bed, there are two bronze plaques engraved with Gene's name, one awarding him as Engineer of the Year from the Engineer's Country Club in 1987 and the other from the New York State Society of CPA's, celebrating his outstanding service. Innumerable people recognize Gene for his lifetime of hard work and success, but you'd be hard-pressed to find someone else who has the pleasure of eating lunch with him twice a week.

AFTERWORD

Over the course of two months, I was adopted by eight grandparents.

Any time I saw them after our interviews, they stopped whatever they were doing—be it beading a necklace during a craft project, reading the newspaper in Town Square, eating lunch in Mustard & Rye, or getting manicures from volunteers—to give me a kiss on the cheek and an update on their lives. They told me who had visited them in the last week, what their plans were for that day, and asked me to update them on my work; who I had interviewed since them, and if I was still enjoying myself.

What I felt was more than enjoyment—it was a deep appreciation for their lifetimes of strength and resiliency.

I hiked with them on the long roads of their stories, up and down the steep hills of financial and family challenges, children being born and children dying before their time. I traveled beside them around tight turns of life-threatening decisions, war-torn unpredictability, and both psychological and physical health crises. I ran with them in the face of danger, often moving two steps behind to watch them persevere alone.

As Herman says in his interview: "I did not think of myself as anything special. I did what I had to do."

We all would benefit from Herman's attitude. Overcoming obstacles is a necessary evil, and approaching our challenges with an unrelenting drive can help us travel our own roads and brace us for our own tight turns.

It was an honor and a privilege to learn from these people, and I will never forget them.

I hope you won't, either.

Madlyn and Leonard
Abramson Center
for Jewish Life^{SM}
CARING FOR GENERATIONS

Madlyn and Leonard Abramson Center for Jewish Life
A heritage of caring, a tradition of excellence

Who We Are

Compassionate care for the aged. Steadfast support for families and caregivers. Comforting, homelike living environments. Pioneering approaches to service delivery. Strong partnerships with our community. Commitment to Jewish life and learning.

These are the hallmarks of the Madlyn and Leonard Abramson Center for Jewish Life – a leader in caring for the Jewish aged for over 140 years.

At the Abramson Center for Jewish Life we have changed and grown with our community, but our mission has remained constant: to enhance the quality of life of seniors through superior care, education and research.

Since 1866, the Abramson Center and its predecessor agencies have supported our communities most vulnerable citizens, the aged, providing them, with unique living environments, enlightened care, companionship, educational and cultural enrichment, and a continuous connection to their Jewish heritage.

As a nonprofit, Jewish-sponsored organization, we have long served as a safety net for Jewish seniors in need of long-term care who have no financial means. Today, we continue our mission with services for seniors residing on campus as well as those living throughout Greater Philadelphia.

Throughout our commitment to excellence, we are helping to raise the standards in eldercare in our community and nationwide.

Our mission is to enhance the quality of life of seniors by providing exceptional care in innovative living environments, assisting family caregivers, and by answering important questions about aging through research. We are committed to continuing our historic role in serving the Jewish community and to our distinguished heritage of honoring our elders.

Madlyn and Leonard Abramson Center for Jewish Life
1425 Horsham Road
North Wales, PA 19454
www.abramsoncenter.org
215-371-1800

ABOUT THE AUTHOR

Drew Feith Tye graduated from the University of Pennsylvania in May 2009 with a B.A. in Jewish Studies and a minor in Creative Writing. Her poetry has been twice published in the *Penn Review*, University of Pennsylvania's premiere literary and visual arts magazine. *Here And Not Forgotten: Stories of a Wiser Generation* is her first book. Tye lives in Philadelphia, Pennsylvania.

www.ingramcontent.com/pod-product-compliance
Lightning Source LLC
Chambersburg PA
CBHW031254280526
45784CB00004B/1857